Oscar on the moon

Words by PEGGY BLAKELEY   Paintings by TAXI KITADA

ADAM & CHARLES BLACK · LONDON

I'd like to tell you about my friend Oscar.
Oscar is a flea
and my mum doesn't much like fleas—
but she puts up with him
because we are such good friends.
Can you see him on the edge of my book?
He always likes to be near me when
I am doing something.
I was reading a story.

The story in my book was about a flea
who went to see the King and Queen
and got a medal for doing something extraordinary.
And he didn't even take a bite out of the Royals
as fleas often do when they meet people.

There's no doubt about it,
Oscar was very impressed
by the flea in the story
who'd done something extraordinary.
And he decided that he'd do something
to make him famous
so that he could have a story
written about him.
'I know,' said Oscar,
'I'll go with the man
who's going to the moon.
That should make me famous.'

So Oscar packed his little bag
and smuggled himself on to a jet
that was going to America.
He greatly enjoyed the flight
especially when he jumped
from passenger to passenger
taking tasty little bites
as he went along.
He could be a very mischievous little flea.

At last he arrived at
Cape Kennedy and
Apollo 11 was just
about to be launched.
'I'll find myself an
astronaut and wiggle
into his space suit,'
said Oscar.
And this he did.

After four days speeding through the sky
which seemed to take forever
the space ship landed on the moon.
The hatch was opened, the steps lowered
and Oscar leapt out.
He beat the astronaut to it
and he was first on the moon.
Imagine that, the very first.

What's more, Oscar appeared on television.
I know because I saw him.
He was sitting on the astronaut's shoulders
bold as brass and waving a little flag
and looking very pleased with himself.
What an adventure!

And what a fuss there was
when Oscar and the astronaut landed safely back on earth.
There were parades through the streets
when everybody cheered
and television interviews and all sorts of excitement.
Oscar had done something extraordinary at last.
He was the first flea on the moon.

When all the excitement had died down
and Oscar had had his fun
he decided to come home to me.
He stowed away on a helicopter
and floated down on a parachute to land near my house.
I think he was quite glad
to creep into my room again
and he had such a lot to tell me.

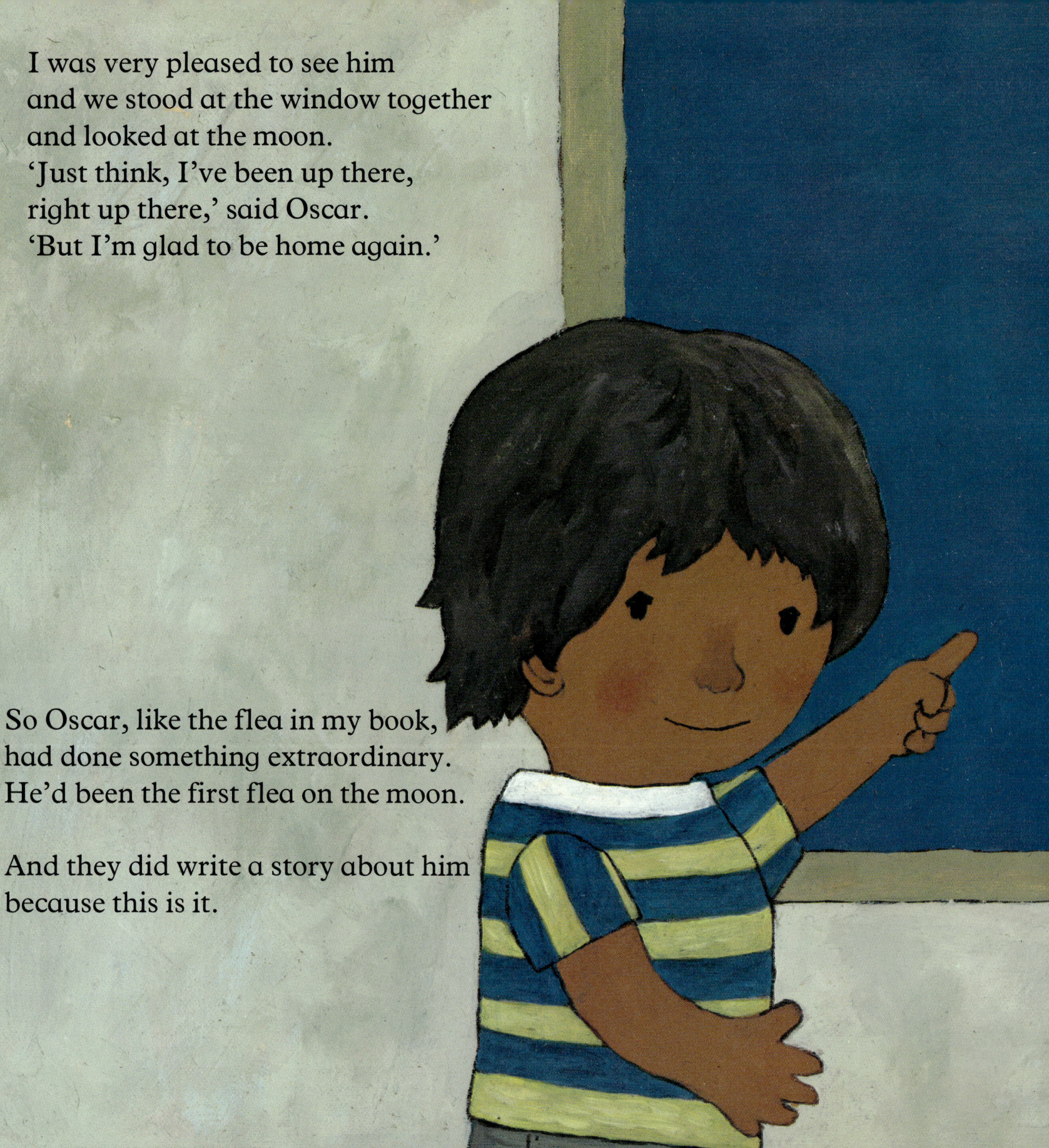

I was very pleased to see him
and we stood at the window together
and looked at the moon.
'Just think, I've been up there,
right up there,' said Oscar.
'But I'm glad to be home again.'

So Oscar, like the flea in my book,
had done something extraordinary.
He'd been the first flea on the moon.

And they did write a story about him
because this is it.

The READ TOGETHER Books
by Peggy Blakeley

Boy on a Hill Top
The Runaway Tram
Clouds
Holes
Neighbours
Jake
That Kind of Rabbit
Another Day Tomorrow
James and the Model Aeroplane
Emmie and Chips
I Bet I Could
The Little Shepherd Boy
The Day I Got Better
Rain
Oscar on the Moon
The Smallest Christmas Tree

A & C Black (Publishers) Limited
35 Bedford Row, London WC1R 4JH

First published in Japan by Shiko-sha Company Limited
Printed in Japan

© Original by Tamao Fujita

ISBN 0 7136 2090 0